Better Homes and Gardens®

AT THE CIRCUS

Hi! My name is Max. I have some great projects to show you—and they're all about the circus! We're going to have lots of fun making them together.

©Copyright 1991 by Meredith Corporation, Des Moines, Iowa.
All Rights Reserved. Printed in the United States of America.
First Edition. First Printing.
Library of Congress Catalog Card Number: 90-63297
ISBN: 0-696-01932-9
MAX THE DRAGON™ and MAX™ and the WILLOW TREE PALS™
and other characters in this book are trademarks and copyrighted
characters of Meredith Corporation, and their use by others is strictly prohibited.

Inside You'll Find...

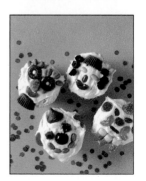
2

Under the Big Top

The circus is about to begin in the tent called the Big Top. But the show can't start until some missing flags are found. Look at the 3 red flags on top of the tent. Can you find 6 white flags and 5 other red flags hidden in the picture?

Circus Tent

Making and playing with a three-ring circus is lots of fun. Watch your clothes-pin circus friends perform amazing feats under your Big Top. Help them tumble. Help them fly. What else can they do?

What you'll need...

- Big Top (see page 30)
- Crayons, markers, or colored pencils
- Stickers (optional)
- Tape
- Scissors
- One 9x12-inch piece of construction paper
- White crafts glue
- 1 toothpick
- Wooden clothespins
- Glitter, pompoms, beads, or buttons
- Yarn

1 Decorate your Big Top any way you like. Turn your Big Top so the decorated side is on the bottom. Fold up the triangular sides (as shown).

2 Tape together the points of 2 opposite triangles (as shown). Tuck the points of the 2 remaining triangles under the taped points.

3 For the flag, fold a small piece of paper in half. Cut out a triangle with one side on the fold. Unfold. Glue the toothpick along the fold (as shown). Fold. Attach to Big Top.

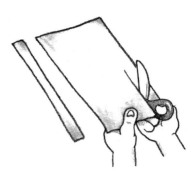

4 To make circus rings, cut three 1-inch-wide strips from the long side of the construction paper (as shown). Decorate the strips any way you like.

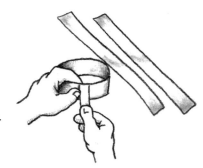

5 Tape the ends of 1 strip together to make a circle (as shown). Repeat for the 2 remaining paper strips. Place the 3 circus rings inside your Big Top.

6 For each circus performer, draw a face on a clothespin. Decorate the clothespin any way you like. For hair, glue yarn to the clothespin or attach a construction-paper hat (as shown).

Big Top Nibble Mix

Peanuts! Popcorn! Candy! Max loves to eat while he watches the circus. Here's a yummy treat you can make using his favorite circus snacks. Just put everything in a bag and shake it up.

What you'll need...

- One 1-gallon heavy-duty sealable plastic bag or paper sack
- Measuring cups
- 4 cups popped popcorn
- 1 cup peanuts
- 1 cup animal crackers
- 1 cup candy-coated milk chocolate pieces

1 Open the plastic bag. Put the popcorn, peanuts, animal crackers, and candy-coated milk chocolate pieces into the bag (see photo).

2 Close the end of the bag and seal. Shake the bag to mix well (see photo). Open carefully and scoop up a handful and eat.

Amazin' Raisin Nibble Mix

This treat tastes great anytime—and it's good for you, too. For Amazin' Raisin Nibble Mix, use 4 cups popped popcorn, 1 cup peanuts, 1 cup round toasted oat cereal, and 1 cup raisins. Mix everything in a bag just as you would for Big Top Nibble Mix.

Snacks For Sale

Zany Clowns

These silly clowns are putting on a rip-roaring, side-splitting show for Max and the gang. Can you count the number of clowns in the show?
Which clown do you think is the funniest?

Look at the clothes in this box. Find each piece of clothing on 2 different clowns.

Funny Clown Bows

Pretend you are a clown
And wear a bow that's big and bright.
All your friends will laugh and giggle
Because you are a silly sight.

What you'll need...

- One 7x12-inch piece
  tissue paper,
  gift wrap, or
  construction paper
- Ruler
- Tape
- 1 pipe cleaner

1 Place the tissue paper on the work surface so one of the long sides is closest to you. Make a fold on a long side ½ inch from the edge. Press hard to make the fold stay in place.

Turn the paper over and make another fold about ½ inch from the first fold (see photo). Turn and fold again and again until all the paper is folded.

2 Wrap a piece of tape around the center of the folded paper. Unfold the ends to make the bow.

Bend the pipe cleaner into the shape of the letter C. Tape the center of the pipe cleaner to the center of the bow (see photo).

Wear the bow around your neck as a clown's bow tie or in your hair as a headband.

Silly Clown Shoes

Feel like clowning around? Make a pair of these oversized shoe-box shoes and you'll start off on the right foot. Ask your Mom or Dad for an old jacket, hat, and tie to complete your costume.

What you'll need...

- 20 gummed paper reinforcements (optional)
- 2 Clown Shoes (see page 31)

- Two 60-inch lengths of ribbon or yarn or two 60-inch shoe laces

- 2 pot scrubbers or pompoms (optional)

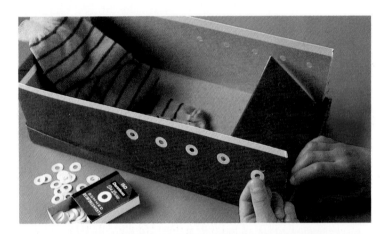

1 If you like, lick and stick the paper reinforcements over the punched holes on each of the Clown Shoes (see photo). This creates eyelets on your Clown Shoes just like the ones on your sneakers.

Fold the front end of each shoe down into the box.

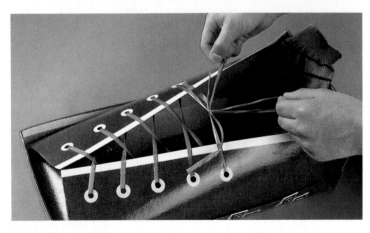

2 For each shoe, thread 1 ribbon through the 2 eyelets at the end of the shoe. Lace the shoes, threading the ribbon through the holes and crossing in the center. Pull the ribbon firmly to fold down the sides. (For pot scrubber decorations shown on page 15, see page 31.)

Tie the ends of the ribbon in a bow (see photo).

Crazy Clown Cakes

Clowns can be silly or sad or happy. But all clowns try to make you laugh. Think of the funniest clown you ever saw. What did the clown do to make you laugh? Create a funny clown face on a cupcake.

What you'll need...

- Table knife or narrow metal spatula
- 1 can vanilla frosting or Butter Frosting (see page 31)
- 16 cupcakes (not frosted)
- Assorted candies, raisins, and dried fruit bits

1 Use the table knife to spread frosting on the top of each cupcake (see photo).

2 To make a clown face, press candies into the frosting for eyes, a nose, and a mouth.

If you like, add more candies for hair, a collar, or a hat. Repeat with the remaining cupcakes.

Birthday Party Favors

Celebrate your birthday with a circus party. For take-home party favors, let your guests make Crazy Clown Cakes.

Give a cupcake, frosting, and candy to each guest. Let each guest create a funny face.

Dazzling Performers

Gus and Ernie steal the show when they swing on the flying trapeze. Look closely at the two pictures. They are not exactly alike. Can you find the 10 things that are different?

Flying Trapeze Performer

Imagine flying through the air. That's what a trapeze performer does. It takes years and years of practice and training to become one. Here's a paper trapeze artist that flips as you twirl the trapeze.

What you'll need...

- One 9x12-inch piece of construction paper
- Crayons or markers
- Scissors
- Tape
- 2 pipe cleaners
- White crafts glue
- Glitter, small buttons, or sequins
- 1 plastic drinking straw or 1 pencil

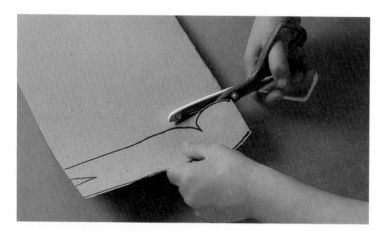

1 Fold the construction paper in half crosswise. For the head, draw a circle with the top of the circle on the folded edge. Draw the body below the circle.

Cut out the head and body cutting through both thicknesses of paper (see photo). One side will be the front of your trapeze artist and the other will be the back.

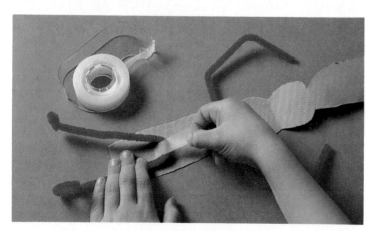

2 On the front, draw a face and hair. Draw more hair on the back. Unfold the body.

For arms, bend one pipe cleaner to look like the letter C. For legs, bend the other pipe cleaner to look like the letter V. Tape the legs and arms to the inside of the body (see photo). Tape the back and front pieces together.

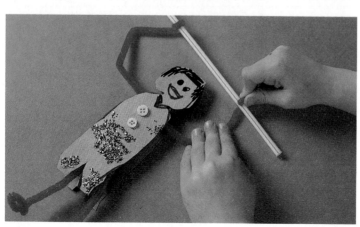

3 For the costume, draw designs on the body. Dab a small amount of glue onto the body. Sprinkle with glitter. Shake off excess glitter. Glue buttons on the body. Let dry.

Bend the hands around the drinking straw (see photo). Hold the straw at both ends and twirl the straw to flip the trapeze artist.

Magnificent Megaphone

Ringmasters run the circus shows. A long time ago, ringmasters talked through megaphones. A megaphone, like a microphone, makes your voice louder. Make your own megaphone and pretend you are a ringmaster.

What you'll need...

- Scissors
- One 9x12-inch piece of construction paper
- Crayons, markers, or colored pencils
- Tape or white crafts glue
- Buttons (optional)
- Rickrack (optional)

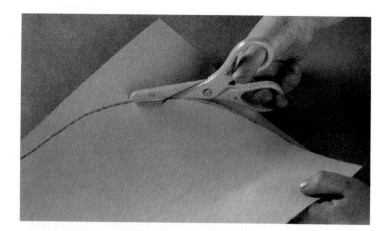

1 Cut a 9-inch square from the construction paper. Save both pieces. With a crayon, draw a line to round off one corner of the square (see drawing on page 31). Cut along the line (see photo).

Draw designs on the paper cutout.

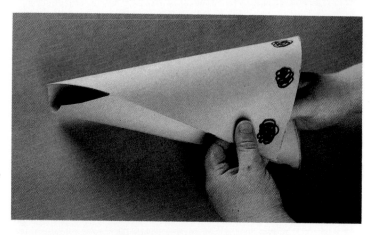

2 Bring the sides of the paper cutout together to make a cone shape (see photo). Tape the edges together.

If necessary, cut off the tip of the cone to make an opening you can talk through.

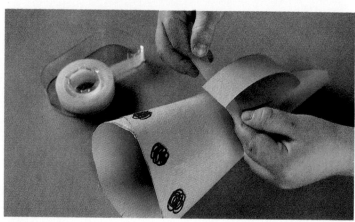

3 If you like, make a handle for your megaphone. Cut a 1x9-inch strip from the remaining piece of construction paper. Tape the ends together.

Make 2 creases in the ring so that 1 side of the ring is flat. Tape the flat side of the ring to the megaphone (see photo).

If you like, glue buttons and rickrack to the megaphone.

Fancy Megaphones

Here are some more ideas
for your megaphone:
● Use sequins, glitter, yarn,
ribbon, or circus stickers to
decorate your megaphone.
● For a handle, poke a hole
in the cone with the end of
a pipe cleaner. Bend the
end of the pipe cleaner on
the inside to hold it in
place. Repeat with the other
end of the pipe cleaner.

Amazing Animals

Max is in charge of the circus parade. Can you help him keep track of the animals? Count the elephants, birds, leopards, tigers, monkeys, dogs, seals, lions, bears, and horses.

Did You Know...

- Circus animals are trained to respond to signals. When the animal sees the trainer's hand move or head nod, the animal knows to perform a trick.
- Monkeys make great circus stars because they love to play and they think doing tricks is playing.

- In addition to being in circus acts, elephants sometimes help set up the circus by moving heavy equipment.
- Many circus animals are born in the circus. Their mothers and fathers are circus performers, too.

Roaring Big Cats

Grrrrr! Grrrrr! Watch out for the lions, tigers, and leopards. Make your own big cat with a pop-up tongue and giant-size teeth.

What you'll need...

- One 6x9-inch piece of red construction paper
- Crayons
- Scissors
- Big Cat Face and Nose (see page 32)
- White crafts glue
- Markers or tempera paints (optional)
- Buttons or paper eyes
- 3 pipe cleaners, cut in half (optional)

1 For the mouth, fold the red construction paper in half. Make a tight fist with your hand and put your fist on top of the paper with your wrist even with the fold. With a crayon, trace around your fist (see photo). Cut out the mouth.

2 Draw a tongue on the remaining red paper. Cut out the tongue. Make a small fold at one end of the tongue.

Open up the Big Cat Face. Glue the mouth to the center of the inside. Glue the folded edge of the tongue to the mouth (see photo). For the teeth, draw or paint white dots around the edge of the mouth. Let dry.

3 Glue the flap on each end of the Big Cat Nose to the face. Glue buttons onto the face for eyes. Draw the whiskers or glue pipe cleaners to either side of the Big Cat Nose for whiskers.

Draw the ears above the eyes. For a tiger, draw stripes on your Big Cat Face (see photo). For a leopard, draw spots, and for a lion, draw hair for a mane.

Elephant Headdress

Make this elephant headdress and pretend you are an elephant. You are bigger than all the other animals. You have floppy ears, a long trunk, and huge tusks.

What you'll need...

- Four 2¼x12-inch strips of construction paper
- Crayons, markers, or colored pencils
- Scissors
- Tape
- One 9-inch paper plate or one 9-inch paper circle
- Ruler
- One 9x12-inch piece of construction paper (optional)

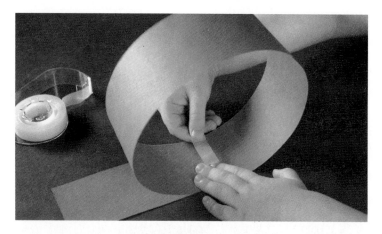

1 For the headband, lay 2 of the construction paper strips end to end. Tape these two ends together to make one long strip.

Then, wrap the long strip around your head. Ask an adult to mark with a crayon where the strip overlaps. Remove the strip. Tape the ends of the long strip together at the pencil mark (see photo).

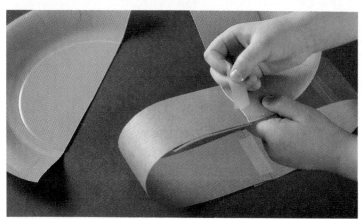

2 For the ears, cut the paper plate in half. Tape one ear in place on each side of the headband (see photo). Fold the ears forward where you attached them to the headband. If you like, draw eyes on the headband.

3 For the trunk, with adult help, tape together the 2 remaining paper strips end to end. Make a fold ½ inch from the edge. Turn the paper over. Make another fold ½ inch from the first fold. Turn and fold until all the paper is folded. Tape to the headband (see photo). If you like, cut tusks from construction paper and tape to the band.

Did You Know...

- Elephants are among the smartest of the circus animals.
- An elephant's trunk is really its nose. A trunk has more than 40,000 muscles, so it can pick up a peanut or uproot a tree.
- The largest elephant ever seen in the circus weighed 6½ tons (more than 3 cars) and was named Jumbo.

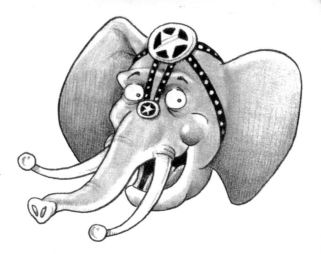

Under the Big Top

See pages 4 and 5

You and your children will find out a lot more about the circus at your local library. Look for both fiction and non-fiction books.

● Reading Suggestions:
Inside the Circus
by Frank Fitzgerald
Circus!
by Jack Prelutsky
Curious George Goes to the Circus
Edited by Margaret Rey

Circus Tent

See pages 6 and 7

Our kid-testers had many ideas to make the performers stand up straight. Ask your children to cut out shoes from construction paper and to glue them to the bottom of the clothespin. Or, press the clothespin performers into balls of modeling clay. Or, fold a piece of cardboard or poster board to use as a stand for the performer.

Before your children start this project, you'll need to make the Big Top:

Big Top: On a large piece of poster board or brown krafts paper draw the Big Top using the pattern below. Cut out the Big Top.

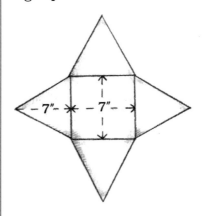

Big Top Nibble Mix

See pages 8 and 9

Since children love the circus, give your child's birthday party a circus theme. Pack this easy-to-fix snack into colorful paper bags or cardboard boxes for party favors. If you like, decorate the bags or boxes with circus stickers.

Zany Clowns

See pages 10 and 11

If your children love to laugh at clowns, bake this yummy clown cake. This fun cake is perfect for birthday parties.

Hot Milk Sponge Cake

  1 cup all-purpose flour
  1 teaspoon baking powder
  ¼ teaspoon salt
  2 eggs
  1 cup sugar
  ½ cup milk
  2 tablespoons margarine
     or butter

    Butter Frosting (see recipe, page 31) or
  1 package creamy white frosting mix (for 2-layer cake)
    Food coloring
  1 large red gumdrop

● Grease and lightly flour 2 ovenproof 1-quart glass mixing bowls; set aside.
● Mix flour, baking powder, and salt; set aside.
● In another bowl beat eggs with an electric mixer on high speed 4 minutes or till thick. Gradually add sugar; beat on medium speed for 4 minutes more. Add flour mixture to egg mixture; stir just till mixed.
● In a saucepan heat and stir milk and margarine till margarine melts. Stir into batter and mix well. Pour half of the batter into each prepared bowl.
● Bake in a 350° oven about 35 minutes or till a wooden toothpick comes out clean. Cool in bowls on wire racks for 10 minutes. Remove cakes from bowls; cool on racks.
● Spread the flat side of one cake with some of the Butter Frosting. Top with the other cake, flat side down. Frost entire cake.

• To decorate the face, use food coloring to tint the remaining frosting as desired. Use a decorating bag and tips to apply a clown face and hair. Press the gumdrop into frosting for nose. Add a paper party hat and bow tie. Serves 10.

Funny Clown Bows

See pages 12 and 13

Children, clowns, and imaginary play are a perfect match. To help your children look the part, paint their faces to look like clowns. Here's how:
• Apply zinc oxide salve to the child's face to make a white base. Zinc oxide salve is available at pharmacies and theatrical shops.
• With red lipstick, apply a large mouth. Then, outline the mouth with an eyeliner pencil.
• Use an eyeliner pencil to draw eyebrows.
• With rouge or lipstick, make a circle on each cheek.
• Draw a diamond or a square around each eye with an eye shadow pencil or lipstick.
• Don't use wax crayons, felt-tip markers, or any type of paint for makeup. These materials may irritate skin.

Silly Clown Shoes

See pages 14 and 15

At least one day before your children make this project, assemble the shoes.

Clown Shoes: Collect 2 shoe boxes, scissors, a hole punch, 2 old socks, and a strong household glue (such as model airplane glue).

For each shoe, use scissors to cut the corners of one end of the box from top to bottom. Fold the end flap into the box.

Using the hole punch, punch 5 holes on each of the long sides. Start punching at the cut end and punch the

fifth hole at the middle of the box. Place the lid upside down on the work surface. Glue the bottom of the shoe to the inside of the lid. Glue the sock into the shoe box (see page 14, photo 1). Let dry overnight.

For the pot scrubber decoration shown in the photo on page 15, thread each length of ribbon through a pot scrubber before your child begins to lace the shoes.

Crazy Clown Cupcakes

See pages 16 and 17

For cupcakes, prepare batter for Hot Milk Sponge Cake (see recipe on page 30). Pour into 16 paper-lined muffin cups. Bake in a 350° oven for 20 to 25 minutes or till a wooden toothpick comes out clean. Remove from pans; cool on racks. Frost with Butter Frosting.

Butter Frosting

   6 tablespoons margarine
      or butter
4½ to 4¾ cups sifted
      powdered sugar
   ¼ cup milk
1½ teaspoons vanilla
• Beat margarine with an electric mixer on medium speed till light and fluffy. Gradually add *half* of the powdered sugar, beating well.
• Beat in milk and vanilla. Gradually beat in the remaining powdered sugar. Then, if necessary, beat in additional milk to make the frosting spreadable. Makes 2 cups.

Dazzling Performers

See pages 18 and 19

Circus performers talk about kinkers and grunsels. Do you know what these words mean? Here are some words to add to your vocabulary:
Fancy pants: the ringmaster
Grunsel: a child
Joey: a clown
Kinker: any circus performer
Painted pony: zebra
Stripes: tigers

Flying Trapeze Performer

See pages 20 and 21

Ask your children to make a trapeze artist to resemble each member of your family. Explain that many circus acts are performed by families. The children learn their skills from their parents. Encourage your children to use their imagination and make up trapeze acts with their paper family.

Magnificent Megaphone

See pages 22 and 23

This project was a hit with our kid-testers. We found the megaphone has a nicer shape if you round off one corner of the square (see drawing below). It's best if you draw this line so your children know where to cut.

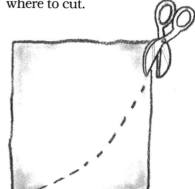

Amazing Animals

See pages 24 and 25

Do you know how animal trainers make tigers, elephants, and other animals perform tricks?

The trainers encourage the animals with love, trust, and patience. Although trainers may use whips or guns in their acts, they do not harm the animals. The sound of whips or guns gets the animals' attention. The whips don't touch the animals and the guns just make noise.

● Reading Suggestion: *Randy's Dandy Lions* by Bill Peet

Roaring Big Cats

See pages 26 and 27

You need to provide 2 construction paper cutouts for each roaring cat project.

Big Cat Face: Fold a 4½x9-inch piece of construction paper crosswise in half. Cut only one side of the folded paper as shown below.

Big Cat Nose: Draw and cut out the nose as shown below. Fold in half lengthwise. Fold under a small flap on each side of the Big Cat Nose.

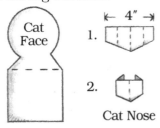

Cat Face

1.

← 4″ →

2.

Cat Nose

Circus Party Invitations

These big cat cards are just the right size for invitations to a circus party. Or, you also can decorate them to look like kittens or puppies.

Remember to include the date; beginning and ending times; your name, address, and phone number; and an R.S.V.P. request.

Elephant Headdress

See pages 28 and 29

Here's another elephant project you and your children can make together. The children can cut out these crunchy elephant-shaped treats with cookie cutters. Then, they can decorate them with candy.

Chocolate Circus Critters

Margarine or butter
½ cup butterscotch pieces
½ cup semisweet chocolate pieces
¼ cup light corn syrup
2 tablespoons margarine or butter
3 cups crisp rice cereal
Assorted decorations (red cinnamon candies, shoestring licorice, candy corn, gumdrops, raisins, candied cherries, mixed dried fruit bits, and/or nuts)

● Line a baking sheet with waxed paper. Grease the paper with margarine. Set aside.

● In a heavy medium saucepan heat butterscotch pieces, chocolate pieces, corn syrup, and 2 tablespoons margarine till melted, stirring constantly. Remove from heat and stir in cereal till evenly coated.

● Turn onto prepared baking sheet. Pat into a 12x6-inch rectangle. Chill about 15 minutes or till slightly firm.

● Cut the chilled cereal mixture into elephant and other animal shapes with cookie cutters. Decorate with assorted decorations.

● Chill till firm. Wrap each animal in clear plastic wrap. Store in refrigerator. Makes about 6.

BETTER HOMES AND GARDENS® BOOKS

Art Director: Ernest Shelton   Managing Editor: David A. Kirchner   Family Life Editor: Sharyl Heiken

AT THE CIRCUS

Editors: Sandra Granseth and Mary Major Williams   Graphic Designers: Harjis Priekulis and Linda Vermie
Project Manager: Liz Anderson
Contributing Illustrator: Buck Jones
Contributing Photographer: Scott Little

Have BETTER HOMES AND GARDENS® magazine delivered to your door.
For information, write to: ROBERT AUSTIN, P.O. BOX 4536, DES MOINES, IA 50336